SARAH MICHELLE GELLAR

A Real-Life Reader Biography

Phelan Powell

Mitchell Lane Publishers, Inc.
P.O. Box 619
Bear, Delaware 19701

First Printing

Real-Life Reader Biographies

Selena	Robert Rodriguez	Mariah Carey	Rafael Palmeiro
Tommy Nuñez	Trent Dimas	Cristina Saralegui	Andres Galarraga
Oscar De La Hoya	Gloria Estefan	Jimmy Smits	Mary Joe Fernandez
Cesar Chavez	Chuck Norris	Sinbad	Paula Abdul
Vanessa Williams	Celine Dion	Mia Hamm	Sammy Sosa
Brandy	Michelle Kwan	Rosie O'Donnell	Shania Twain
Garth Brooks	Jeff Gordon	Mark McGwire	Salma Hayek
Sheila E.	Hollywood Hogan	Ricky Martin	Britney Spears
Arnold Schwarzenegger	Jennifer Lopez	Kobe Bryant	Derek Jeter
Steve Jobs	Sandra Bullock	Julia Roberts	Robin Williams
Jennifer Love Hewitt	Keri Russell	**Sarah Michelle Gellar**	Liv Tyler
Melissa Joan Hart	Drew Barrymore	Alicia Silverstone	Katie Holmes
Winona Ryder	Alyssa Milano	Freddie Prinze, Jr.	Enrique Iglesias
Christina Aguilera			

Library of Congress Cataloging-in-Publication Data
Powell, Phelan.
     Sarah Michelle Gellar/Phelan Powell.
         p. cm. — (A real-life reader biography)
     Includes index.
     ISBN 1-58415-034-3
     1. Gellar, Sarah Michelle, 1977- —Juvenile literature. 2. Actors—United States—Biography—Juvenile literature. [1. Gellar, Sarah Michelle, 1977- 2. Actors and actresses. 3. Women—Biography.] I. Title. II. Series.
PN2287.G46 P68 2000
792'028'092—dc21
[B]
                                                             00-034932

ABOUT THE AUTHOR: Phelan Powell is a freelance writer who has written several books for young adults. Her titles include biographies of John Candy, Tom Cruise, John LeClair, and Hanson (Chelsea House), and Jeff Gordon and Garth Brooks (Mitchell Lane). A former newspaper reporter, Phelan lives just outside Philadelphia, PA with her husband and two sons.

PHOTO CREDITS: cover: Archive Photos; p. 4 Corbis; p. 8 Globe Photos; p. 22 Globe Photos; p. 24 Globe Photos; p. 27 Archive Photos; p. 30 Globe Photos

ACKNOWLEDGMENTS: The following story has been thoroughly researched, and to the best of our knowledge, represents a true story. While every possible effort has been made to ensure accuracy, the publisher will not assume liability for damages caused by inaccuracies in the data, and makes no warranty on the accuracy of the information contained herein. This story has not been authorized nor endorsed by Sarah Michelle Gellar.

Table of Contents

4

Chapter 1
Sarah as Sarah

What does a vampire slayer do when she goes home? If you said, "Anything she wants," you would be right. Sarah Michelle Gellar, popular star of the TV show "Buffy the Vampire Slayer," has entered the new millennium as an independently wealthy woman. She has worked very hard to get where she is today.

But aside from her wealth, Sarah, who is now in her early twenties, is just a very nice young lady. She is totally comfortable with the fame that 20 years of work in commercials, television and

Sarah has starred in commercials, television, and film for nearly 20 years.

movies has brought her. "I'm tired and I complain sometimes, but this is my career and I love it," Sarah once said.

Always a go-getter, Sarah has never waited for roles to come to her. Before one project is finished, she usually has something else to work on waiting in the wings.

Sarah describes herself as a work-aholic.

Sarah describes herself as a workaholic, someone who needs to work more than anything else. This has not been a bad thing for the young beauty who got her first job when she was just out of diapers.

"I think I get places because of my brains and my intelligence and my talent. I never think about my looks," she says.

Her millions of fans do, though. But on any given night, Sarah is as likely to be watching reruns of "Seinfeld" while she's eating her favorite food, pasta.

Like many of television's young stars, Sarah has her own house, which sits in a very private section of the

Hollywood Hills area. She lives with her rabbit, Harley, and dog, Thor, and loves to watch any movie that stars her favorite actor, Tom Cruise.

Although her fans would love to know more about the off-screen Sarah, just like everyone else, she needs her own space.

She makes herself as available as possible to reporters for interviews, but actually hates being interviewed. When Sarah became the star of "Buffy," she knew that interviews, photo shoots, and appearances would be necessary to make sure the show would have a big audience.

Sarah soon found herself booked on the most popular talk shows in the country, including "Live! with Regis and Kathie Lee," "MTV Live" and "Late Night with David Letterman." Sarah even got her own "Got Milk?" magazine ad, which always features the best-known celebrities.

It is not hard to imagine that Sarah could have her pick of boyfriends. She

She lives with her rabbit and her dog in the Hollywood Hills area.

likes to keep her private life private, though. Sarah has gone out with such stars as Freddie Prinze, Jr. and "Friends" star Matt LeBlanc.

Celebrity spotters are likely to find Sarah hanging out at Starbucks or the Hard Rock Café, or sunning herself on the sunny beaches of Aruba or

Sarah starred with Ryan Phillippe in Cruel Intentions.

Bermuda when she takes a much-needed vacation.

Sarah has earned quite a magnificent life for herself. Even her mother never dreamed of the wonderful future in store for her new baby when Sarah was born in 1977.

Chapter 2
Work Is Fun!

Exciting things are always happening in a city as big and bustling as New York. Something really big happened April 14, 1977. Rosellen and Steven Gellar were the proud parents of Sarah Gellar, a little bundle of joy who would soon be seen by television viewers across the country.

Most children spend time wondering what they are going to be when they grow up. This tiny brown-haired tot started her career when she was just four years old. In later years Sarah would remember feeling like an adult in a miniature body when she was a child.

Sarah Gellar was born on April 14, 1977.

Sarah's flashing green eyes and ready smile caught the attention of a television person one day. Sarah and her mother were having a nice lunch in a local restaurant. The man who saw them was a casting agent. His job was to find people he thought would be good actors for a new movie that was being made for television.

When the agent saw Sarah chattering and smiling away with her mom, he suddenly forgot all about his lunch and quickly walked up to Sarah's table. Sarah did not understand everything her mother and the man talked about, but he was very nice and her mother was really excited.

When the man left, Sarah's mom told her she had a chance to be an actor on television. Sarah could hardly believe her ears! But she knew it was something she absolutely wanted to do.

When she was older, Sarah told *Soap Opera Magazine,* "Acting was in my blood from the time I was little. I was this big ham, and I had to do something!

Sarah's flashing green eyes and ready smile caught the attention of a casting agent.

So I would perform for anyone who would listen or watch. I would put on little plays or act out movies."

Sarah's life had been that of a normal girl being raised in the big city. The noise, the people, the lights, the stores, all seemed to fill Sarah with a special energy that made her want to stand out and be noticed. Soon after the lunch at that restaurant, Sarah found herself with her mother waiting on a snowy island!

Sarah was going to play the daughter of a character played by famous actress Valerie Harper in a movie called *Invasion of Privacy*. Sarah never had any problem saying anything to anybody. She found it very easy to remember the words she was supposed to say and to act like somebody else's daughter. For her, the hardest part of this first acting job was to keep her teeth from chattering.

"We did the filming on an island in the winter, and it was freezing," Sarah remembers. "I was really little—I mean I

Sarah's first acting job was in the film *Invasion of Privacy* with Valerie Harper.

was four, but also small for my age—and there was so much snow, they hired this guy to carry me on the set because they were afraid I'd get lost in a snowdrift."

When Sarah watched *Invasion of Privacy*, she thought it was wonderful to see herself on television. She knew what she wanted to be when she grew up! The great thing about Sarah's shot at television was that lots of theatrical agents were watching the movie, too.

The next thing she knew, Sarah's mother told her she had another job, and this one was big! Sarah was five years old and in a Burger King commercial! Every kid she knew had been to Burger King, and now she was the one on TV telling them to go! Sarah already was becoming used to the world of a working girl. Burger King signed her to do thirty more commercials.

When she started working, Sarah would wait for her name to be called to begin the day's shooting. At the sound of "Sarah Gellar," she would be on her feet, and with a quick kiss to her mom, set off to do her job.

After a couple of months of work, Sarah had to decide whether to join a union. A union is a group of people who do the same kind of work. The union helps to see that people are treated fairly.

No two actors can have the same name when they join the actors' union. It turned out there was already a woman named Sarah Gellar in the union. Sarah decided then that she wanted to be called Sarah Michelle Gellar. The union record-keeper solemnly wrote down Sarah's new name. Sarah crossed her fingers behind her back, hoping her new special name would bring her good luck.

When Sarah joined the actor's union, she had to add "Michelle" to her name.

Chapter 3
Nothing but the Best

Sarah enjoyed working on "Spenser: For Hire."

A little girl could not be luckier, but maybe her middle name did add that extra star quality. It seemed as soon as Sarah finished one project, someone would call with another job for her to do. Sarah could turn down work, but that is something she hardly ever did. She loved working. It made her feel very important and good about herself.

Sarah worked on the television series "Spencer: For Hire." She remembers the star of the show, Robert Urich.

"I was just eight or nine years old, and he was just wonderful to me,"

Sarah recalls. Urich knew that sometimes things are hard for child actors, who sometimes miss out on the things their friends at home are doing.

One of Sarah's early projects was a part in a Broadway play, *The Widow Claire*. Being in a play is a very different and wonderful experience for an actor. Acting on Broadway is something most people can only dream about. Sarah loved performing in front of a live audience. Two of Sarah's fellow actors in the play quickly became her best friends: Matthew Broderick and Eric Stoltz.

All the glamour and excitement of television and the stage were absolutely wonderful, of course. But Sarah did have to go to school like every other child she knew. She first attended Columbia Preparatory, a private school. It was not the best time of her young life. It was hard for Sarah to make friends because she had to work so much. Hardly any of her classmates had to juggle a career and a social life, as she

Sarah attended private school while she pursued a career in acting.

did. "After school and on the weekends, I had to choose between going out with all the kids or going to auditions," she said. "The second you start missing school and social events, you stop getting invited to parties, and people stop talking to you."

As time went on, Sarah found herself on casting calls or at auditions with some of the same faces. She became close friends with other young actors and actresses who lived a life like hers. Two of her close friends in grade school were Melissa Joan Hart, who is best known now for her starring role in the TV show "Sabrina, the Teenage Witch," and Jenna von Oy, who starred in the show "Blossom." Sarah always had a special time with Melissa because Melissa had six brothers and sisters. When Sarah and her mother joined the Hart family after work, it was like a party.

Sarah always focused on the good feeling she would get when she was working on a project. It was as if she was made to do this one thing. But work is not all Sarah did. Her mom was concerned that Sarah have all the opportunities of a normal childhood. One thing she did not have for a while was a dad.

When Sarah was seven, Steven and Rosellen Gellar were divorced. Unfortunately, Sarah and her dad were not close. But when her mom remarried later, Sarah found a good friend in her stepdad.

Sarah's favorite sports are still ice-skating and football. When Sarah started ice-skating competitively as a child, she won third place in the New York State regionals. Sarah could never just *do* something—she always had to do it to the best of her ability.

Sarah was always tiny for her age. But no one would ever want to give her a hard time. When she was eight years old, Sarah began to take tae kwon do, a martial art similar to karate. There was something so intense and satisfying about the workouts that Sarah stayed

Sarah also ice-skated com— petitively as a child.

Sarah practiced tae kwon do until she was nineteen.

with the martial art until she was nineteen.

Most of the kids in her tae kwon do class were boys. All the girls she knew were at dancing classes. Sarah wanted a more vigorous challenge. "I placed fourth in the Madison Square Garden Karate Championships," she told a reporter.

Sarah spent a lot of time practicing martial arts in elementary school. The tae kwon do discipline has helped her in every area of her life. That help was something Sarah really needed when she entered the choppy waters of her teen years.

Chapter 4
Cleaning Up in the Soaps

Since Sarah had worked most of her life, there was no question that she would continue to attend private schools. But, Sarah learned success was no guarantee of happiness. Her few years at the LaGuardia Junior High School were absolutely miserable. But when work called, Sarah happily answered.

Sarah is particularly proud of a project she did when she was fourteen. She had a small part in a TV movie about the life of the late Jacqueline Kennedy Onassis, wife of the former president, John F. Kennedy. Three

At LaGuardia Junior High School, Sarah was miserable.

different actresses were needed to play Onassis during her lifetime. Millions of viewers watched the show about this nationally admired woman.

Sarah's happiness about that role must have been an omen for more good things to come. The very next year, Rosellen remarried and Sarah immediately felt like she was a member of a regular family.

Sarah got her high school diploma in two-and-a-half years.

Sarah could have done commercials for the next school she attended, New York City's Professional Children's School. Finally, she had found a place where she could relate to kids who lived as she did, trying to balance work and school on a regular basis.

Sarah attacked her high school classes the way she approached everything else in her life, with a dazzling vigor. The amazing teen got her high school diploma in two and a half years.

Sarah's secret? She was disciplined enough to tell herself to do homework first each day after school, and then memorize her lines for her current role.

When she was fifteen, Sarah landed her first regular TV show. "Swans Crossing" was one of the first television shows written for teenagers. The kids who spent so much time watching TV had a show they could really relate to. The show tried to focus on all the things that teenagers face, both good and bad. Sarah played Sydney Rutledge, a rich and spoiled brat who caused the nicer characters a lot of grief.

Sarah played in sixty-five episodes of "Swans Crossing." The show was then cancelled. However, a bigger-than-ever part was waiting for Sarah.

Sarah had always been a soap opera fan. She loved to watch the tangled web of relationships play out on the television screen each day. Then, Sarah was asked to audition for a spot in one of the most famous of all daytime dramas, "All My Children."

Her first regular TV show was "Swans Crossing."

From left to right: Kristen Mahon, Sarah Michelle Gellar, Carisa Dahlbo, and Kristy Barbera from "Swans Crossing"

"Soaps are an amazing training ground," she said. "There's nothing like them; unlike theater, there's a new script every day. The amount of work you do on a soap cannot be compared to anything else—how little time you have to prepare for the huge amount of actual work."

In 1993, Sarah started playing the daughter of the character played by the famous soap actress, Susan Lucci. Lucci, for years, had played one of the nastiest women in the soaps. Fans loved how well she played the role of Erica Kane. Sarah was written into the show to play the part of the long-missing daughter of the wicked woman. Sarah's character, Kendall Hart, was to be every bit of a problem to the quiet TV town of Pine Valley as her mother was.

Looking back, Sarah found the most challenging part of this great opportunity was that no one told her exactly how bad Kendall was supposed to be. She was not told that her character was the daughter of Erica Kane.

"I didn't know when I auditioned for Kendall that she would turn out to be [so nasty]. I had heard rumors, but they were squelched very quickly."

Even though she had been a professional for a long time, this lack of information made Sarah uneasy the first day on the set.

"I was very nervous. I kept thinking, 'What if I'm really bad and

On "All My Children," Sarah played Kendall Hart, the daughter of Erica Kane, played by Susan Lucci.

*Sarah played
the scheming
Kendall Hart
on "All My
Children."*

they fire me?'" Sarah said. After all, this was the big time.

"On my first day, I walked in and snuck in the back behind the coffee machine to watch Susan and Michael Nader rehearse a scene. All of a sudden Susan said, 'Hold it, we need to stop for a minute,' and she walked over to me and said, 'Congratulations! I'm very glad you're here.' Then she introduced me to everyone. She really helped me and always made sure I was okay during my first couple of weeks."

"[Susan] really helped me and made sure I was okay during my first couple of weeks."

Chapter 5
Saving
the World

Sarah received a Daytime Emmy award before Susan Lucci.

Sarah enjoyed great success in her role on "All My Children." She played a very believable Kendall Hart and the audience loved her. But after three years, Sarah grew tired of being on the soap opera. Rumors started flying around that Sarah's TV mom was a little upset at all the attention the young and talented Kendall Hart was getting. Sarah was nominated for a Daytime Emmy for Outstanding Younger Actress in a Daytime Drama in 1994.

For years, Susan Lucci had been nominated for a Daytime Emmy but she had never won the award. In 1995 Sarah was again nominated in the same category, and this time she walked off the award stage hugging the trophy.

Sarah as Buffy the Vampire Slayer.

Lucci once again was nominated but did not win.

It was clear to Sarah that the time had come to move on.

Sarah's next role would be her most challenging. She was to keep the world safe from the threat of some very real vampires.

"Buffy the Vampire Slayer" began as an idea. It then was turned into a movie in 1992. The movie was a box-office

bomb. Something had not clicked. The writer wanted the audience to be scared, but not too scared. The movie ended up just being goofy and not very interesting.

But eventually some people in television picked up the idea again and wanted to do a series about a teenage girl who hunts vampires. Two big questions had to be answered. Who would be the perfect actress with looks, brains, athleticism, and courage to get the audiences interested in her struggles? Could scripts be written that would be true to teenagers, depicting a teen's everyday struggles?

Sarah loves her Buffy character.

The answer to both questions, happily, was yes. When Sarah was on "All My Children," her makeup man saw the *Buffy* movie and realized Sarah resembled the actress who played the lead. He suggested she audition for the TV role. She did, and won the part.

Sarah loves her *Buffy* character. In an online interview, Sarah once wrote, "She [Buffy] doesn't fit in. She doesn't know if she wants to be a cheerleader or fight vampires—and that's what makes her so interesting and believable. Buffy is a person who is lost, and who doesn't know where she belongs. And you feel for her."

Sarah particularly relates to Buffy because, like the vampire slayer, Sarah always had to choose between work and doing things with her friends.

It took a while for the TV show to reach the air, but in March 1997 the first episode was broadcast. Sarah jumped into the role with her usual heads-up attitude.

After the first season, Sarah began to get calls for movie auditions. A box-office horror hit, *I Know What You Did Last Summer*, featuring Sarah and Jennifer Love Hewitt, opened in theaters in October 1997. Teens flocked by the millions to scream at the screen.

Sarah filmed *Scream 2* next, which opened that same year in December. The busy actress next appeared in *Cruel Intentions* and *Simply Irresistible*.

She has starred in several teen horror movies, including *Scream 2*.

Portia DeRossi, Rebecca Gayheart, and Sarah Michelle Gellar in Sream 2.

In March 1998 Sarah won the Blockbuster Entertainment Award for the Best Supporting Actress: Horror Category for her part in *I Know What You Did Last Summer*. Maybelline, the multimillion dollar makeup company, signed Sarah to become a spokeswoman in their television commercials and magazine ads in August 1999.

No one knows how long Buffy will be charged with the task of slaying vampires instead of going on a special date, but one thing is for sure: Wherever the celebrity spotlight is, Sarah Michelle Gellar will be there.

Selected Filmography

Cruel Intentions (1999)
Simply Irresistible (1999)
Small Soldiers voice (1998)
"Hercules" TV series, voice (1998)
Scream 2 (1997)
I Know What You Did Last Summer (1997)
"Buffy the Vampie Slayer" TV series (1997-present)
"Beverly Hills Family Robinson" TV movie (1997)
"All My Children" TV series (1993-1995)
"Swans Crossing" TV series (1992)
"A Woman Named Jackie" TV miniseries (1991)
"Girl Talk" TV series (1989)
High Stakes (1989)
Invasion of Privacy TV movie (1983)

Chronology

- Born April 14, 1977, in New York City
- Cast in a TV movie, *Invasion of Privacy*, at the age of four
- At five, appears in a commercial for Burger King
- 1988, Sarah's parents divorce
- Plays the young Jacqueline Kennedy Onassis in the TV miniseries, *A Woman Named Jackie*, 1991
- 1992, appears in the short-lived TV drama "Swans Crossing"
- Beginning in 1993, Sarah plays the part of Kendall Hart on the soap opera "All My Children." She stays on the show for three years and wins a Daytime Emmy for Outstanding Younger Actress in a Drama
- Sarah appears in the hit TV series "Buffy the Vampire Slayer" beginning in 1997
- 1997, stars in *I Know What You Did Last Summer* and *Scream 2*
- 1999, stars in the movies *Cruel Intentions* and *Simply Irresistible*
- 1999, becomes a spokeswoman for Maybelline cosmetics
- 2000, continues in her role as Buffy, the Vampire Slayer

Index